First World War
and Army of Occupation
War Diary
France, Belgium and Germany

58 DIVISION
175 Infantry Brigade
London Regiment
2/9 Battalion
4 February 1917 - 31 January 1918

WO95/3009/3

The Naval & Military Press Ltd
www.nmarchive.com
Published in association with The National Archives

Published by

The Naval & Military Press Ltd

Unit 10 Ridgewood Industrial Park,

Uckfield, East Sussex,

TN22 5QE England

Tel: +44 (0) 1825 749494

www.naval-military-press.com

www.nmarchive.com

This diary has been reprinted in facsimile from the original. Any imperfections are inevitably reproduced and the quality may fall short of modern type and cartographic standards.

© Crown Copyright
Images reproduced by permission of The National Archives, London, England, 2015.

Contents

Document type	Place/Title	Date From	Date To
Heading	WO95/3009/3 2/9 London Reg.		
Heading	War Diary Of 2/9th London Regt From 4/2/17 To 28/2/17		
War Diary	Harve	04/02/1917	05/02/1917
War Diary	Avil-Le-Chateau	06/02/1917	06/02/1917
War Diary	Warens	07/02/1917	08/02/1917
War Diary	Sub-St-Leger	09/02/1917	13/02/1917
War Diary	Burles & Bienvillers	14/02/1917	18/02/1917
War Diary	Grenas	19/02/1917	26/02/1917
War Diary	Guadiempre	27/02/1917	28/02/1917
Heading	War Diary Of 2/9th Bn London Regt. (Q.V.R's) From 1st March 1917 To 27th March 1917		
War Diary	Sector F1	01/03/1917	05/03/1917
War Diary	Sector D2	06/03/1917	17/03/1917
War Diary	Blaireville	18/03/1917	27/03/1917
Heading	War Diary Of 2/9th Battn London Regt (Queen Victoria Rifles) From 28th March 1917 To 25th April 1917 Volume 1		
War Diary	Berles Au Bois HQ. at W22d 60 40	28/03/1917	05/04/1917
War Diary	Busles Artois	06/04/1917	09/04/1917
War Diary	Miraumont	10/04/1917	14/04/1917
War Diary	Achiet Le Petit	20/04/1917	25/04/1917
Heading	War Diary 2/9th Bn. London Regt. From 26/4/17 To 26/5/17 Volume 4		
War Diary	Achiet Le Petit	26/04/1917	03/05/1917
War Diary	Favreuil	04/05/1917	05/05/1917
War Diary	Lagnicourt	06/05/1917	12/05/1917
War Diary	Favreuil	13/05/1917	15/05/1917
War Diary	Bihucourt	16/05/1917	20/05/1917
War Diary	Noreuil	21/05/1917	21/05/1917
War Diary	Bullecourt	22/05/1917	25/05/1917
Heading	War Diary Of 2/9th London Regiment From 26th May To June 30th 1917 Volume 5		
War Diary	Ecoust	26/05/1917	27/05/1917
War Diary	C29 Mory	28/05/1917	03/06/1917
War Diary	Bullecourt	03/06/1917	09/06/1917
War Diary	Ecoust	09/06/1917	14/06/1917
War Diary	Mory	15/06/1917	24/06/1917
War Diary	Logeast Wood	25/06/1917	30/06/1917
Heading	War Diary Of 2/9th Battn London Regiment From 1st July To 31st July 1917 Vol. 1		
War Diary	Logeast Wood	01/07/1917	05/07/1917
War Diary	Bancourt	06/07/1917	06/07/1917
War Diary	Ytres	07/07/1917	07/07/1917
War Diary	Havrincourt	08/07/1917	16/07/1917
War Diary	Havringcourt Wood	17/07/1917	19/07/1917
War Diary	Rauyalcourt	20/07/1917	22/07/1917
War Diary	Havringcourt	22/07/1917	27/07/1917
War Diary	Dainville	28/07/1917	31/07/1917

Heading	War Diary Of 2/9th Battn London Regiment (Queen Victoria's Rifles) From 1st Aug 1917 To 31st Aug 1917 Volume 7		
War Diary	Dainville	01/08/1917	23/08/1917
War Diary	Brake Camp	24/08/1917	28/08/1917
War Diary	Brown's Camp	29/08/1917	29/08/1917
War Diary	Dambre Camp	30/08/1917	31/08/1917
Heading	War Diary Of 2/9th Battalion London Regiment (Queen Victoria's Rifles) From 1st Sep 1917 To 30th Sep 1917 Volume 1		
War Diary	Dambre Camp	01/09/1917	02/09/1917
War Diary	Canal Bank	03/09/1917	05/09/1917
War Diary	St Julian	06/09/1917	10/09/1917
War Diary	Canal Bank	11/09/1917	11/09/1917
War Diary	Query Camp	12/09/1917	20/09/1917
War Diary	Reigersburg Camp	21/09/1917	22/09/1917
War Diary	Canal Bank	23/09/1917	25/09/1917
War Diary	Cluster Houses	26/09/1917	28/09/1917
War Diary	Reigersburg Camp	29/09/1917	30/09/1917
Miscellaneous	2/9th Battalion London Regiment (Queen Victorias Rifles)		
Heading	War Diary Of 2/9th Battalion London Regiment (Queen Victoria's Rifles) Period From 1st October 1917 To 31st October 1917 Volume 1		
War Diary	Reigersburg Camp	01/10/1917	01/10/1917
War Diary	Listergaux	02/10/1917	21/10/1917
War Diary	Road Side Camp	22/10/1917	31/10/1917
Heading	War Diary Of 2/9th Battn London Regiment (Queen Victoria's Rifles) From 1st November 1917 To 30th November 1917 Volume 1		
War Diary	Siege Camp Transport Lines	01/11/1917	02/11/1917
War Diary	Canal Bank	03/11/1917	04/11/1917
War Diary	Kempton Park	05/11/1917	08/11/1917
War Diary	Siege Camp	09/11/1917	14/11/1917
War Diary	Purbrook Camp	15/11/1917	17/11/1917
War Diary	Petworth Camp	18/11/1917	27/11/1917
War Diary	Coulomby	28/11/1917	30/11/1917
Heading	War Diary Of 2/9th Battn London Regiment (Queen Victoria's Rifles) Volume 1 Period From 1st December 1917 To 31st December 1917		
War Diary	Coulomby	01/12/1917	06/12/1917
War Diary	Siege Camp	07/12/1917	10/12/1917
War Diary	Kempton Park	11/12/1917	16/12/1917
War Diary	White Mill Camp	17/12/1917	24/12/1917
War Diary	Kempton Park	25/12/1917	29/12/1917
Heading	War Diary Of 2/9th Battalion London Regiment (Queen Victoria's Rifles) From 1st January 1918 To 31st January 1918		
War Diary	In The Line	01/01/1918	01/01/1918
War Diary	Bridge Camp	02/01/1918	07/01/1918
War Diary	Houtkerque	08/01/1918	19/01/1918
War Diary	Proven	20/01/1918	20/01/1918
War Diary	La neuville	21/01/1918	31/01/1918

WO 95
3009/3

2/9 London Reg

CONFIDENTIAL

WAR DIARY
of
2/9th Bn. London Regt

from
4/2/17 to 28/2/17

Vol 1. 58

Army Form C. 2118.

WAR DIARY
or
INTELLIGENCE SUMMARY. 1/5 **N. Staff. Regt**

(Erase heading not required.)

Instructions regarding War Diaries and Intelligence Summaries are contained in F.S. Regs., Part II. and the Staff Manual respectively. Title pages will be prepared in manuscript.

Place	Date	Hour	Summary of Events and Information	Remarks and references to Appendices
Havre	4-2-17	1 am	Disembarked from transport "La Marguerite" and marched to Rest Camp	
Havre	5-2-17	9 am	Left Rest Camp and entrained at Havre Station	
Achiet-le-Vullens	6-2-17	2 pm	Detrained at Achiet-le-Chateau, marched to billets at Wavens	
Wavens	7-2-17		In billets at Wavens.	
—	8-2-17		Move from Wavens to billets at Sus-St-Leger	
Sus St Leger	9-2-17			
	10-2-17		Billets at Sus-St-Leger. Battalion in Training	
	11-2-17			
	12-2-17			
	13-2-17		Transport & Stores moved to Henu. Bn. moved to Burles. Billets for night.	
Burles & Bienvillers	14-2-17		Went into trenches 104th to 129th for instruction. A & B Coys with 5/4 N. Staff. Regt. at Bienvillers. C & D Coys with 5 S. Staff. Regt. at Burles. Bn HQ 5/4 N. S. Staff Regt.	
	15-2-17		Instruction continued. A & B with 5/4 N. Staff Regt. C & D with 5/4 N. S. Staff Regt.	
Bienvillers	16-2-17			
	17-2-17		Left trenches & proceeded to billets. A & B Coy to Bienvillers & C & D Coy at Burles.	
	18-2-17		Move from Burles & Bienvillers to billets at Grenas. Taken over from 1/5 Bn. Lincoln Regt. Transport moved from Henu to Grenas	

(1)

T2134. Wt. W708—776. 500000. 4/15. Sir J.C. & S.

Army Form C. 2118.
2 July AFA 2042

WAR DIARY
or
INTELLIGENCE SUMMARY
(Erase heading not required.)

Sheet II

Place	Date	Hour	Summary of Events and Information	Remarks and references to Appendices
GRENAS	19.2.17 20.2.17 21.2.17 22.2.17 23.2.17 24.2.17 25.2.17		In billets at GRENAS. Battalion Training. Anti-Gas Test.	
	26.2.17	10 a-	Move from GRENAS to billets at GUADIENPRÉ. Move from GUADIENPRÉ to billets at RIVIÈRE in relief of 1/6 Bn. W.Riding Regt. A Coy proceeded to WAILLY and relieved A Coy of 1/6 Bn. W.Riding Regt in keep.	
GUADIENPRE	27.2.17			
	28.2.17		One to Sub Sector E1 in relief of 1/5 Bn. W. Riding Regt. relief completed 3 p.m.	

A R Dunn
Lt. Col. Cmdg.
2/9 Bn. London Regt.
(Queen Victoria Rifles).

Vol 52

Confidential

War Diary of
2/4th Bn London Regt (Q.V.R.)

From 1st March 1917 to 27th March 1917.

Volume 1

Army Form C. 2118.

WAR DIARY
or
INTELLIGENCE SUMMARY
(Erase heading not required.)

2/9th London Regt

Instructions regarding War Diaries and Intelligence Summaries are contained in F. S. Regs., Part II. and the Staff Manual respectively. Title Pages will be prepared in manuscript.

Place	Date	Hour	Summary of Events and Information	Remarks and references to Appendices
SECTOR F1	1-3-17		Occupation of trenches Sector F1.	P.6. 2.P.
	2-3-17		ditto	P.6. 2.P.
	3-3-17		ditto	P.6. 2.P. P.6. 2.P.
	4-3-17	3pm	Relieved by 2/10th Bn London Regt. went into Reserve, occupying its original Billets in RIVIÈRE. Remainder in billets there.	P.6 2P
	5-3-17		Remainder in billets there.	
	6-3-17		"C" & "D" Coys. went into dugouts in RIVIÈRE	P.6. 2.P.
		3.3 pm	"A" & "B" Coys remaining	
			Bn of London Regt. in trenches Sector D 2	
	7-3-17		Remainder in conversation in trenches Rivière	P.6. 2.P.
SECTOR D2	8-3-17		ditto ditto	P.6. 2.P.
	9-3-17		ditto	P.6. 2.P.
	10.3.17	1pm	C, D + ½ HQ Coys occupied trenches relieving A & B & ½ HQ Companies, who returned to billets at RIVIÈRE & GROSVILLE	P.6. 2.P.
	11.3.17		Occupation of trenches Sector D2	P.6.
	12.3.17		ditto	P.6.
	13.3.17		ditto	P.6.
	14.3.17	1pm	A, B & ½ HQ Coys occupied Trenches relieving C, D & ½ HQ Companies, who went to billets in RIVIÈRE & GROSVILLE.	P.6.
	15.3.17		Occupation of the above D 2 SECTOR.	P.6.
	16.3.17			P.6.
	17.3.17			P.6.

2449 Wt. W14957/M90 750,000 1/16 J.B.C. & A. Forms/C.2118/12

Army Form C. 2118.

WAR DIARY
INTELLIGENCE SUMMARY

2/9th Bn London Regt

(Erase heading not required.)

Instructions regarding War Diaries and Intelligence Summaries are contained in F. S. Regs., Part II. and the Staff Manual respectively. Title Pages will be prepared in manuscript.

Place	Date	Hour	Summary of Events and Information	Remarks and references to Appendices
BLAIREVILLE	18.3.17	2.15am	Our patrol (officer + 22 men) entered enemy front + support lines. Several fires were burning in BLAIREVILLE	B.L.
		4 a.m.	Occupation of enemy trenches by C.Coy sent patrols in village. A+B Coys occupied village itself.	
		6 a.m.	D Coy's HQ in reserve at D2 Sector. D Coy moved into BLAIREVILLE	
		4 pm	A+B Coy occupied BLAIREVILLE	
		10 pm	A Coy withdrew from BLAIREVILLE to billets at RIVIÈRE. B Coy withdrew from BLAIREVILLE to billets at GOUY nr L.E.	
	19.3.17	9 a.m.	A+B Coys moved up to BLAIREVILLE remaining 2/9 Mid Coys to D2 Sector. Battalion engaged in salvaging trenches	S.D.
	20.3.17		B.n engaged in salvage work	S.D.
	21.3.17		ditto	
	22.3.17		B.n moved to La CAUCHIE via BASSEUX - BAILLEULVAL - BAILLEULMONT.	
	23.3.17		B.n moved to BERLES au BOIS. rest into billets	
	24.3.17		B.n employed working our road MONCHY - BIENVILLERS. reported at front E.6.a.2.4.	
			gassed from 9 am to 3 p.m. under R.E. supervision. L.G. squad use + Bombing (instructional) Schools started	
	25.3.17		Lt-Col H.B. LIBERTY died at 11.5 pm. A.B.+D. + H.Q. Coys moved to RAVINE. H.Q. at W.22.d.60.40. C Coy remained in BERLES	
			School in BERLES continued	
	26.3.17		Work on MONCHY - BIENVILLERS road continued.	
	27.3.17		ditto. Funeral of Lt-Col H.B. LIBERTY at 11.30 a.m.	
			at SOLERNEAU.	

D.E. Lany Major
O.C. 2/9th London Regt

SH 3

Confidential

War Diary

of

2/9th Batt'n London Reg't (Queen Victoria's Rifles)

from 28th March 1917 to 25th April 1917

(Volume 1)

WAR DIARY
INTELLIGENCE SUMMARY

Army Form C. 2118.

2/9th Bn. London Regt.

Place	Date	Hour	Summary of Events and Information	Remarks and references to Appendices
BERLES AU BOIS Hqrs at Wizzelles	28.3.17	9.30 am & 2.30 pm	Bn engaged mending roads in MONCHY VILLAGE.	W.P.W.
"	29.3.17	8.30 am & 2.30 pm	Bn engaged mending roads in MONCHY VILLAGE, BERLES AU BOIS – RANSART RD	W.P.W.
"	29.3.17		at ADINFER WOOD.	
	30.3.17	9 am	A Coy. on light duty. + 4 Coy. moved to BELLACOURT CHATEAU. C Coy - 100 O.R. + 3 officers	W.P.W.
		11.30 am	to ARRAS. 25 O.R. + 1 officer to DAINVILLE. Remainder of Bn awaiting instruction.	
	31.3.17	8.15	The Bn less 2 Companies moved to AGNY. On arrival there found no billets available	W.P.W.
			& onwards march to AGNEZCHATEAU.	
	1.4.17	3.0	The Bn less A + C Coys moved to trenches E of WAILLY, with HQ at R.23.b.7.5.	W.P.W.
	2.4.17	5.30	The Bn less A + C Coys moved as follows. HQ + B Coy at BEAUMETZ. D Coy at BRETENCOURT.	W.P.W.
	3.4.17	9.30 pm	13 4 Coys C Coy moved in motor lorries to ST AMAND. C Coy moved from ARRAS	W.P.W.
			& DAINVILLE to ST AMAND, whole Bn was in billets by 6 am. 4/4/17	
	4/4/17		Rested in ST AMAND.	W.P.W.
	5/4/17	4.0 pm	Bn marched to B/S LES ARTOIS today. Arrived B. LES ARTOIS at 4.50 pm. work	W.P.W.
			billets	
B/S LES ARTOIS	6/4/17		Battd HQ. B + D Coys + part of HQ Coy. All Coys accupicated + helmets inspected	W.P.W.

WAR DIARY
or
INTELLIGENCE SUMMARY.
(Erase heading not required.)

Army Form C. 2118.

Place	Date	Hour	Summary of Events and Information	Remarks and references to Appendices
BUS LES ARTOIS	7/4/17		Bathed C Coy & remainder of H.Q. Coy. Each half A,B & D sent out working party — relieved, but afterwards cancelled	
BUS LES ARTOIS	8/4/17		Church Parade except A by that started for MIRAUMONT at 7.30 am. Marched — Left BUS LES ARTOIS at 9.5 am. With B² less A Coy, & went into "billets" in MIRAUMONT forming A Coy. 72 men & Lt HODGKINSON left at BUS LES ARTOIS.	17.2.7.11 17.2.2.11
"	9/4/17		A Coy working under Town Major — R.C.D. Coys Traing for Offensive Action. W.S.L.	
MIRAUMONT	10/4/17		Ditto " 30 O.R. arrived from BUS.	W.S.L.
"	11		" B C + D Coys each supplying a	
"	12		Party of 100 men for work on Railway 1½ & 4 miles from ACHIET LE GRAND 2 Officers Italy, 2 O.R. fly by parachute under 2 Lt PENNIE to aq walling. B C + D Coys 9 — 10.30 am Traing in Offensive Action	11.12.11
"	13		by Coys. 10.30 — 1. Training under Coy arrangements. 16 men left with from BUS. Town L.G. Teams & D Coy trained in drill by Sgt BRIGGS. Instruction in German Gunnery by Lt Samuelson. Men washing by Coys in tubs, toin etc	
"	14		A Coy under Town Major. Then ACHIET LEGRAND B/S. Each day supplying 100 men for work on Railway, near ACHIET LEGRAND. 2 O.R. returned from BUS.	11.1.1.11

Army Form C. 2118.

2/9th Bn
London Regt

WAR DIARY
or
INTELLIGENCE SUMMARY.
(Erase heading not required.)

Instructions regarding War Diaries and Intelligence Summaries are contained in F. S. Regs., Part II. and the Staff Manual respectively. Title pages will be prepared in manuscript.

Place	Date	Hour	Summary of Events and Information	Remarks and references to Appendices
ACHIET LE PETIT	20/4/17 (continued) 21/4/17		Instruction in signalling continued. Coy parades for instruction in Outpost work, Shelter fld day reported at 9 a.m. to Hqs 3rd Corps Trch Supply School ACHIET LEGRAND. School continued.	N.P.W. 11.2.M N.P.W.
"	22/4/17	9 a.m.	B Coy paraded for divine service 1145. B Coy paraded for practice attack on LOG EAST farm.	N.P.W.
"	23/4/17	9 a.m.	C+D Coys training in Outpost work. Allways working parties - A Coy reported to 313 R.E. (instruction) 65 at at 9.10. C.9. C.57. c. N.W.(1500) at 9 a.m. B Coy to R.T.O. Movement at 9 a.m. C Coy to R.T.O. ACHIET LEGRAND at 4 pm. School continued as per as provis. A+B. Coys working under R.T.O at ACHIET LEGRAND. C Coy training.	N.P.W. 11.2.M
"	24/4/17 25/4/17		B Coy kit inspection, Bayonet fighting. Physical drill etc.	N.P.W. 11.2.M

A.N.Walker Lieut
adj
2/9th 15th London Regt

75/38

War Diary Vol 4
2/9th Bn London Reg.t
from 26.4.1917 to 26/5/1917

Volume 4

WAR DIARY
or
INTELLIGENCE SUMMARY.
(Erase heading not required.)

Army Form C. 2118.

Place	Date	Hour	Summary of Events and Information	Remarks and references to Appendices
Achiet le Petit	26/4/17	10 a.m.	Parade with Company arrangement. Including checking Gun Drill, Artillery formation, Bayonet fighting, and Stationary digging.	O.C.O
		1.45 P.M.	Parade for Advance Guards and Outpost work.	O.C.O
"	27/4/17	6 a.m.	Parade for Close Order Drill. 10.45 Parade for inspection by Brigadier. 1.45 P.M Parade for Brigade attack. Working Parties. C. company reported to R.T.O. MIRAUMONT at 9 a.m.	O.C.O
	28/4/17	10.30 a.m	Coy's inspected by Brigadier. Specialists Training continues. Signallers, Lewis Gunners, & Rifle Grenadiers. Working Parties. B. coy report to R.T.O ACHIET LE GRAND thro'up 28/29 (150 strong) C. coy working with light Railway Operating Coy at ACHIET LE GRAND. Coy billeted there. Q.M. One Platoon D. coy working outside Town Huage ACHIET LE PETIT.	O.C.O
	29/4/17	10 a.m	Parade for Arms Service in Camp. Lewis Gunnery & Bayonet fighting instruction carried on. Working Parties, 8 a.m Two Platoons of D. coy reported to 4th C.R.T. at ACHIET LE GRAND. 8.30 a.m. A. coy working with LG Tramway coy at ACHIET LE GRAND through 29/30 B. coy reported to R.T.O ACHIET LE GRAND.	O.C.O
	30/4/17	8.30	Parade Working Parties. Three coys. ACHIET LE GRAND. B. coy standing by etc. 8 a.m. I.S. 14	O.C.O

Army Form C. 2118.

WAR DIARY
or
INTELLIGENCE SUMMARY.
(Erase heading not required.)

Instructions regarding War Diaries and Intelligence Summaries are contained in F. S. Regs., Part II. and the Staff Manual respectively. Title pages will be prepared in manuscript.

Place	Date	Hour	Summary of Events and Information	Remarks and references to Appendices
ACHIET LE PETIT	1/5/19	9 a.m.	Bn Parade for Arm Drill. 9.30 D. Coy on rifle range. A Coy exercise of anaymene? musketry.	App
"	"	"	Bayonet fighting and Clean Guns Drill. 2.30 Shorts completed on Rifle Range. Shooting continues.	App
"	2/5/19	9 a.m.	D. Coy on Rifle Range. Specialists training continued. Working parties. 8.30 a.m. Term by Train thence MIRAUMONT. 6m by ACHIET LEGRAND. Coy by ACHIET LE PETIT.	App
"	"	"	6m Coy ACHIET LEGRAND. R.T.O. midnight 2/3rd	App
"	3/5/19	11 a.m.	Bn Parade musketry arrangement. Specialist training continues	App

WAR DIARY
or
INTELLIGENCE SUMMARY.
(Erase heading not required.)

Army Form C. 2118.

Place	Date	Hour	Summary of Events and Information	Remarks and references to Appendices
Favreuil	4/5/17		Bn paraded at 1.30 and moved into camp from Achiet-le-Petit	
"	5/		Resting all day. Bn paraded at 6.20 P.M. and moved up to the support line at LAGNICOURT. In support to 11th Bn.	
LAGNICOURT	6/5/-		In support in sunken road S.E. of LAGNICOURT. We had sixteen casualties to-day on Lewis Pipers. Remained two of the occupation to hour dress'd later.	
"	7"		In support. All quiet. Occasional shelling.	
"	8"		Moved up at 9.30 P.M. and relieved 11th Bn in front line.	
"	9"		All quiet on our front. All rations & water were carried up at night as there are no communication trenches. Our Lewis guns QUEANT.	
"	10"		All quiet. Nothing to report.	
"	11"		" " " "	
"	12"		We were relieved by 29th Australian Infantry Bn. Return complete by 2.30 a.m. Bn marched back of Pelling's independently and arrived in camp near FAVREUIL	
FAVREUIL	13"		Resting and cleaning up.	
	14"		Resting	

WAR DIARY
or
INTELLIGENCE SUMMARY.
(Erase heading not required.)

Army Form C. 2118.

Place	Date	Hour	Summary of Events and Information	Remarks and references to Appendices
FAVREUIL	15/5/17		Company training till 11 a.m. inclusive "Musketry", "Physical Drill".	
"	"	2 P.M.	Bn. paraded and marched to Camp at BIHUCOURT.	
BIHUCOURT	16/5/17	9.9 a.m. to 12.45 & 2.30 to 4.30 P.M.	Parades under company arrangements to include "Elm Gun Drill", "Bayonet fighting", "Musketry", 2.30 to 4.30 P.M Coy.	
"	"		Bayonet fighting, Musketry and lectures by Platoon commanders. 9.30 P.M till 11 P.M coy. officers were practised in map-reading.	
"	17/5/17	9.9 a.m. to 12.45	Company arrangements. "Elm Gun Drill", "Bayonet fighting", "Musketry", 2.30 to 4.30 P.M. Inspection of Musketry. Lewis gun school continued.	
"	"			
"	18/5/17	9 a.m. to 9.30	Coy. parade for "Physical training". 9.45-a.m. Bn. Parade for Gen. demonstration.	
"	"	2.30 to 3 P.M.	Coy drill. B & C companies 3.0 to 4.45- Wiring and Musketry. 9.15 to 10.30 night patrol under coy arrangements.	
"	"		Lewis gun and Bayonets. School of instruction continued. 9.30-6.12.45 Coy drill, Bayonet fighting.	
"	19"	9 a.m. to 9.30	Company parade for Physical Drill. 2.30 P.M. to 4.30 under coy arrangements. Lewis Gun & Bayonet School continued.	
"	20"	-	Bn. paraded for Church Service at 10 a.m. 1.45 P.M. Bn. paraded and moved up the Transport Lines over ERAUCOURT. 8.30 P.M. Bn. moved into Hd. Reserve line at NOREUIL 11th Bn in front line 12th Bn in Support	

Army Form C. 2118.

WAR DIARY
or
INTELLIGENCE SUMMARY.
(Erase heading not required.)

Instructions regarding War Diaries and Intelligence Summaries are contained in F. S. Regs., Part II. and the Staff Manual respectively. Title pages will be prepared in manuscript.

Place	Date	Hour	Summary of Events and Information	Remarks and references to Appendices
MOREUIL	21/5/1.		Bn in bivouac in sunken road between ECOUST – NOREUIL	6/26
BULLECOURT	22/5/1		Bn relieved 2/7th in front line at BULLECOURT	6/26
"	23/.		Bn. Artly. Bursts from 22.0.6.9. on Regt. to 27.B.2.9. Killed 1 O.R. Wounded 30 O.R.	6/26
"	"		Bn. All quiet except heavy shelling from direction of QUEANT. Wiped 3 O.R. Wounded 3 O.R.	6/26
"	24/.		During night of 24/25, two plns of B coy relieved two plns of A coy in front line, Heavy shelling at intervals during the day. B. H.Q. changed	6/26
"	25/.		to H.Qrs. and moved back to railway embankment. Casualties wounded 10 Officers +18 O.R.	6/26

H. N. Walker

Confidential

War Diary
51st
2/9th London Regiment

From 26th May to June 30th/1917

Volume 5

WAR DIARY
or
INTELLIGENCE SUMMARY

Army Form C. 2118.

Place	Date	Hour	Summary of Events and Information	Remarks and references to Appendices
ECOUST	26/8/17		In Billets in ECOUST.	P.O
"	27/8/17		Moved to Transport lines @ 29 Central	P.O
C29	28/		" in camp at MORY	P.O
MORY	29		In camp Training	P.O
"	30		" " "	P.O
"	31		" " "	P.O
"	1		" " "	P.O
"	2		" " "	P.O
"	3		Moved to Front line BULLECOURT Sector. B Right front A & right support. C Left front D Left support. H.Q. in EMBANKMENT.	P.O
BULLECOURT	4		Saw formation. 2/Lt HARPER + Cpl + 2 patrolled across BOV'S thumb as far as U.22.c.3.5. A dangerous different reconnaissance in bright Moonlight. Reported Strong point at U.22.c central strongly held.	P.O
	5		Same formation. C.O. + General reconnoitred new position on left. A.D. Harrington 2/Lt	P.O

Army Form C. 2118.

WAR DIARY
or
INTELLIGENCE SUMMARY.
(Erase heading not required.)

Instructions regarding War Diaries and Intelligence Summaries are contained in F.S. Regs., Part II. and the Staff Manual respectively. Title pages will be prepared in manuscript.

Place	Date	Hour	Summary of Events and Information	Remarks and references to Appendices
BULLECOURT	June 5		at Vs1 & H.5 etc. Situation continued very quiet. Same formation.	P.O.
	6		do. do.	P.O.
	7		Until 10.30 when BN moved & settled in camp, other shelters in ECOUST & LONGATTE. Mr Shand QM & Sergt Major Sake. have for England on furlough. Battalion disposed as follows:—	P.O.
	8		Bn H.Qrs, H.Q. Company, Dhy H.Q & two platoons / D.Coy were under the church of ECOUST C.2.a.9.3. A Coy H.Qrs & A company in shelters running from S.E. corner of LONGATTE S.about C.2.d.8.0. B.Coy, H.Qrs. & B Company at L'HOMME MORT C.Coy. H.Qrs & C company in cellars in ECOUST & LONGATTE D.Coy. two platoons in large dug out at C.2.a.1.6. Relief was completely carried out by 1am without a casualty. C.O. departed on leave after a conference at 1.20 pm Same formation. No working parties except by day. Men without meer. O.D. Harington 2/Lt	P.O. P.O.
	9			

WAR DIARY
or
INTELLIGENCE SUMMARY.
(Erase heading not required.)

Army Form C. 2118.

Place	Date	Hour	Summary of Events and Information	Remarks and references to Appendices
AUGUST		*(continued)*		
	June 9		commenced. 143rd Bttn. have moved at 11.38 hours. Mainforce strafe the Boch & all quiet & normal on our front. They took on prisoner who gave much information.	O.C.
	10		Quiet formation. All companies working during day & night. Much improvement made on the approaches to B.H.Q. & the new mess, which was inaugurated at lunch time. Our friends of 120th R.I.R. brought here on the way back & bags.	O.C.
	11		Same formation & the two stays in support. All continues working except B.Coy by day & night. Improvement of B.H.Q. mess & approaches still continued. 4th Division defended on Neural & heavy bombardment by 4".H". guns on our left & to from 7 & 9 h.m. Situation quiet & normal.	O.C.
	12		Two prisoners of 119th Regt. brought in about 3 a.m. Both tired of the war & gave themselves up. One or two shells near our B.H.Q. about 4 a.m. Work on mess nearly completed. Several of our own 18/dr shells bursting short on village — an 10" & 12" suffered time detonation otherwise normal. A. D. Harrington 9/1/16	

WAR DIARY or INTELLIGENCE SUMMARY

Army Form C. 2118.

Place	Date	Hour	Summary of Events and Information	Remarks and references to Appendices
ECOUST	June 13		Some formation of future movement	B.O.
	14		Started Artillery very active. H.Q. Divisional Front end of St Helen 40th Bn relieved by 10th Bn 2.15 am Offrs & 40th Bn killed & about one other. Bn. moved MORY by 20th Bde.	P.O.
MORY	15		Much anxiety by Zero not only one casualty D.L. enlarged wounded. Artillery Trench manning & making of & defences	P.O. P.O.
	16		Training in camp (in Tnserie) do	P.O.
	17		do	P.O.
	18		do	P.O.
	19		do	P.O.
	20		Morning. Battalion cut & digging PELICAN TRENCH.	P.O.
	21		Parade by companies at 8.80 am.	P.O.
	22		Coy parade under coy arrangements. All schools will be continued. Parade under coy arrangement to include Clean bren drill, musketry. A coy on Rifle range, also Lewis guns, C coy furnished working party of 50 am to work at MORY	MORY

A.D. Harrington 2/7/17

Army Form C. 2118.

WAR DIARY
or
INTELLIGENCE SUMMARY.
(Erase heading not required.)

Instructions regarding War Diaries and Intelligence Summaries are contained in F.S. Regs., Part II. and the Staff Manual respectively. Title pages will be prepared in manuscript.

Place	Date	Hour	Summary of Events and Information	Remarks and references to Appendices
MORY	Jan 1917 22		B. Coy moved to ERVILLERS to work under 52nd Divl Arty. D. coy found party 31 men under RES to MORY. School continued	
	23		Parade under coy arrangements	
	24		11 a.m. Parade for Divine Service. 2.30 p.m. B. O. worked and moved to camp at LOGEAST-WOOD. Remainder coys A.C.D. coy working on lines at ST LEGER. B. Coy ERVILLERS	
LOGEAST WOOD	25		9.0 a.m. & 12.25 and 2.15 p.m. & 4.45. D coy Parade under coy arrangements, Schools, Lewis gun, Sniping, Signalling and Running classes continued	
	26		Parades & coy reports as Rating class. A.C. & 1 E. LEGER GRAND & moved by truck to HAMEL to work as usual. All schools continued	
	27		All Schools continued. A & C. coy returned to B. at 1 p.m. 3 p.m. all officers attending a lecture by Lt. Colles Jackson on Signalling	
	28		9. a.m. coy Parades including Clan Ordu Drill, Bayonet Fighting & Musketry 11 a.m. Lecture by Superintendent of 1 P.T. & B.F. Three Army to all officers. (M.G.O.C.). School continued	
	29th		A. coy on Rifle Range. 8.30 a.m. & 4.30 p.m. B.C. & B coy 9 a.m. Inspection of clothing by O.C. Coys.	
	30		11 a.m. Coy Order Drill, Musketry, Bayonet Fighting, Massey. 9.15 a.m. & 12.30 p.m. coy Parade = Clan Order Drill. Lecture in the afternoon by Dr Harrington 3 p.m.	

O. D. Harrington

T2134. Wt. W708—776. 500000. 4/15. Sir J. C. & S.

Vol 6

Confidential

War Diary
of
2/9th Batt. London Regiment
(Queen Victoria's Rifles)

From 1st July to 31st July 1917
(Volume 1)

WAR DIARY
or
INTELLIGENCE SUMMARY.
(Erase heading not required.)

Army Form C. 2118.

Place	Date	Hour	Summary of Events and Information	Remarks and references to Appendices
LOG EASTWOOD	July 1st		Bn Parade for Divnl Service at 10.a.m. Brigade then Shrine in afternoon	[illegible]
	2nd		Bn had use of Divisional Baths. Coy parades	
	3rd		Bn paraded for Coy training. A.C. & D coy on "Marching" practice	
	4th		Bn paraded at 9.45 a.m. for inspection by Q.O.C.	
	5th		Bn paraded at 1.30 p.m. for move to BANCOURT	
BANCOURT	6th		Bn moved at 2 p.m. for move to YTRES	
YTRES	7th		Bn moved 6.30 p.m. from camp to take over trenches at HAVRINCOURT	
	8th		Bn relieving Brigade parties. Bn on right Bn front, C coy centre Bn front, D coy [illegible]	
HAVRINCOURT			Left Bn front. A coy in reserve at Coy Copse	
	9th		Bn in front line	
	10th		Relief not prev. coy in front line	
	11th		Relief [illegible]	
			D coy patrols met a German N.C.O.	
	12th		sent. And on surrender By T Renaix	
	13th		Bn in front sheard. Patrols out for ends coy	
	14th			

R.E. Count
Lt Col

Army Form C. 2118.

WAR DIARY
or
INTELLIGENCE SUMMARY.
(Erase heading not required.)

Instructions regarding War Diaries and Intelligence Summaries are contained in F. S. Regs., Part II. and the Staff Manual respectively. Title pages will be prepared in manuscript.

Place	Date	Hour	Summary of Events and Information	Remarks and references to Appendices
HAVRINCOURT	July 15		Bn in front line. Orders rec'd from each coy in front line, no improvements	P.P.B
"	16th		Bn relieved by 2/10 relief completion by 12.30 a.m.	P.P.B
Havrincourt Wood	17th		Bn had use of Baths at METZ, rest of day unin coy arrangement, cleaning equipment etc	P.P.B
"	18th		O.B. & C coy workin in front line from 11 P.M till 9 a.m	P.P.B
"	"		Under coy arrangement Working pwts down in Cart Miyn	P.P.B
"	19th		Bn paraded at 2.P.M. and proceeded by train to RAVRALCOURT and went into billets	P.P.B
RAVRALCOURT	20th		Coy parade for clothing inspection. Lewis gun & P.T.B. Jugrilin shoon commenced	P.P.B
"	21st		Oraders 9.9 a.m until coy arrangement	P.P.B
"	22nd		Bn moved into Rearine on left centre relieving 9/2.B, relief commenced 9 P.M coy his 2 hrs intervn	P.P.B
HAVRINCOURT	23rd		Bn carried out rain in vicinity of MOW.COP. The Prince of Wales has amohy paint5 un tinh	P.P.B
"	"		This afternoon & tricks arrived on carrils chepps	P.P.B
"	23		Bn in Rearine, all coy parties, water parties in front line trenches	P.P.B
"	24th			P.P.B
"	25th		Bn moved into billets for the night at BERTINCOURT	P.P.B
"	26th		Bn moved by train to BAUMETS from Crisnchu to DAINVILLE went Bn over coach	P.P.B
"	27th			P.P.B Bn 3 Bann Lt Bn

Army Form C. 2118.

WAR DIARY
or
INTELLIGENCE SUMMARY.
(Erase heading not required.)

Instructions regarding War Diaries and Intelligence Summaries are contained in F. S. Regs., Part II. and the Staff Manual respectively. Title pages will be prepared in manuscript.

Place	Date	Hour	Summary of Events and Information	Remarks and references to Appendices
DAINVILLE	28/7/15		Bn arrived and cleaned up equipment.	
	29/7/15	16.0	Church & arm service. General clean up.	
	30/7/15		Church with Cq arrangement. C.o. inspection Bn at 6 P.M.	
	31/7/15		Bn paraded at 10.45 a.m. for inspection by Brigadier at 11.30	

T2134. Wt. W708—776. 500000. 4/15. Sir J. C. & S.

No 7

Confidential

War Diary

of

2/9th Battn London Regiment
(Queen Victoria's Rifles)

from 1st August 1917 to 31st August 1917

(Volume 7)

Army Form C. 2118.

WAR DIARY
or
INTELLIGENCE SUMMARY.
(Erase heading not required.)

Instructions regarding War Diaries and Intelligence Summaries are contained in F. S. Regs., Part II. and the Staff Manual respectively. Title pages will be prepared in manuscript.

Place	Date	Hour	Summary of Events and Information	Remarks and references to Appendices
DAINVILLE	1/6/17		Brigade Route March. Route: WAGNONLIEU – DUISANS – GOUVES – WARLUS – DAINVILLE. Cancelled.	Mapsheet 57C.
	2/6/17		D.H.A. Conference. Took use of ARRAS Rifle range. Practice field, grouping 100x, application & rapid 200x. B+C did not fire, owing to weather.	M.S.
	3/6/17		Battalion route march/route as for Brigade march postponed 1/6/17.	M.S.
	4/6/17		Platoon training. NCO's, Signalling, Lewis & map reading classes in afternoon.	M.S.
	5/6/17		Church parade.	M.S.
	6/6/17		Platoon training. NCO's, Signalling, snipers, Lewis, eleven continued. Coy on range.	M.S.
			As 6/6/17. B Coy on range at DUISANS.	M.S.
	7/6/17		Brigade day. Practice attack on old trenches three MAILLY & AGNY.	M.S.
	8/6/17		Platoon training. Classes for signallers, snipers L.G.C.	M.S.
	9/6/17		Brigade Assault at Arms in morning; preceded by presentation of appreciation cards to officers, NCO's & men of the Brigade Recommended for Gallant Actions. Brigade Sports in the afternoon.	M.S.
	11/5/17		Company training. A coy on the rifle range at DUISANS. Brigade Boxing Competition in afternoon.	M.S.
	12/5/17		Church parade.	M.S.

T2134. Wt. W708—776. 500000. 4/15. Sir J. C. & S.

WAR DIARY or INTELLIGENCE SUMMARY

Army Form C. 2118.

Place	Date	Hour	Summary of Events and Information	Remarks and references to Appendices
DAHNVILLE	13/8/17		Company training & specialist classes.	
"	14/8/17		" " " " "	
"	15/8/17		Brigade attack scheme on PETIT CHATEAU area. The Battalion acted as enemy to 2/10, 2/11 and 2/12 Battalions, and made a counter attack on them, covered by smoke.	
"	16/8/17		Attack practice on PETIT CHATEAU area. Cold dinner in the field.	
"	17/8/17		Company training till 1 p.m. The afternoon devoted to training for "Carouel at Arms".	
"	18/8/17		Battalion "Carouel at Arms" on Anzonne ground, MAGNON LIEV.	
"	19/8/17		Church Parade.	
"	20/8/17		Company training, musketry. Trench mortar demonstration & reconnaissance for Divisional Exercise.	
"	21/8/17		175 Brigade acted as enemy in Divisional Exercise on WAILLY-FICHEUX area, & delivered counter attack under cover of smoke. Dinner in the field.	
"	22/8/17		Company training & attack practice.	
"	23/8/17		" " " " "	
BRAKE CAMP	24/8/17		Battalion moved by rail from ARRAS to PROVEN & thence by march route to hutted camp in A30.d.19, arriving in camp at 2.30 a.m. 25th.	
"	25/8/17		Platoon training & reconnaissance by Officers commdg Companies.	
"	26/8/17		Church Parade. Reconnaissance by 5 officers of area near ST JULIEN.	

WAR DIARY
or
INTELLIGENCE SUMMARY.
(Erase heading not required.)

Army Form C. 2118.

Place	Date	Hour	Summary of Events and Information	Remarks and references to Appendices
BRAKE CAMP	27/8/17		Platoon training & conferences on forthcoming operations between Coy, Pl, & Section commanders.	Map 28.
"	28/8/17		Platoon training & inspection of kits, arms & ammunition.	
BROWN CAMP	29/8/17		Battalion moved to BROWN CAMP. Platoon training.	
DAMBRE CAMP	30/8/17		" DAMBRE CAMP. Platoon training.	
"	31/8/17		Company training & practice for attack & raid.	

175/58

Vol 8

Confidential

War Diary

of

2/9th Battalion London Regiment
(Queen Victoria Rifles)

Period from 1st June 1917 to 30 Sept 1917

Volume 1

Army Form C. 2118.

WAR DIARY
or
INTELLIGENCE SUMMARY.
(Erase heading not required.)

Instructions regarding War Diaries and Intelligence Summaries are contained in F. S. Regs., Part II. and the Staff Manual respectively. Title pages will be prepared in manuscript.

Place	Date	Hour	Summary of Events and Information	Remarks and references to Appendices
DAMBRE Camp	1/9/17		Train A and B coy practise the attack formation	
"	2/9/17		Church Parade. Practise attack. Reinforced 2 Cos (A and C) to Canal Bank. YSER Canal	
CANAL BANK	3/9/17		Cleaning up lines	
"	4/9/17		"	
"	5/9/17		Moved forward and took cover at ST JULIAN	
ST JULIAN	6/9/17		During line. B on right front & left. A Support. D Reserve	
"	7/9/17		"	
"	8/9/17		"	
"	9/9/17		"	
"	10/9/17		Relieved in line by 2/12 Bn and marched back to the Canal Bank	
Canal Bank	11/9/17		Cleaning up after instruction. Moved to Query Camp	
QUERY CAMP	12/9/17		Coy training - practising the attack. Inspection for deficiencies	
"	13/9/17		Coy training - practising the attack. " Stretcher bearer drill	
"	14/9/17		Coy training. Spry Formation. mix of Bns	
"	15/9/17		Coy training and Rifle Range	
"	16/9/17		Sunday Church Parade at 10.15 am	
"	17/9/17		Bn Parade for inspection by C.O.	

Army Form C. 2118.

WAR DIARY
or
INTELLIGENCE SUMMARY.
(Erase heading not required.)

Instructions regarding War Diaries and Intelligence Summaries are contained in F.S. Regs., Part II. and the Staff Manual respectively. Title pages will be prepared in manuscript.

Place	Date	Hour	Summary of Events and Information	Remarks and references to Appendices
QUERY CAMP	18/9/17		A.C. & B. coy detachmt. to prepare 9 campns. for Rl Gun. amn. dump	O.M.
	19/9/17		Above issues cont. Supplying training.	O.M.
	20/9/17		H.Q. & part of B coy moved to REIGERSBURG Camp B	O.M.
REIGERSBURG	21/9/17		" " to Canal Bank. All coy reprn.	O.M.
Camp	22/9/17		Cleaning up	O.M.
Canal Bank	23/9/17		Preparation for supplies, transport for pl attack	O.M.
	24/9/17		"	O.M.
	25/9/17		Moved up to Rl Line H.Q. in CLUSTER HOUSES, Parking pl attack tonight	O.M.
Cluster Houses	26/9/17		5.50 am ZERO hour, the Battalion, 58 Divn. in front through H.Q.	O.M.
			We had any with other Battns. throughout. All coy concentrating. Counter attack in evg.	O.M.
			right but soon repulsed.	O.M.
	27/9/17		Counter attack in night — 8/10 transport in support within in front, they having seen enemy	O.M.
	28/9/17		Retired in line by 59 Bn. at 3 a.m. Bn moved to REIGERSBURG Camp arriving all by	O.M.
REIGERSBURG	29/9/17		Reorganzn. 9 companies	O.M.
Camp	30/9/17		Inspection by men. for supplies, as dressed parade	O.M.

2/9th Battalion London Regiment (Queen Victoria's Rifles).

NOTES ON EVIDENCE GIVEN 30-9-17.

Beginning on the left with "D" Coy. Capt. Samuelson stated as follows:-
    Nos. 13 and 14 Platoons leading.
    15 and 16 rear platoons.
At zero hour they went off. I was on the left flank along side VON TIRPITZ farm. The two leading platoons went straight ahead.

No.13 platoon
  No.392358 Rfn. Ellement W.A. states:-
We went off from the tape due east. The first thing we came to was what I understood to be VALE HOUSE. Sgt. Jefferies went forward with the others and I lost them in the mist.
Started with 25 men - 22 men missing and 3 accounted for.

No.14 platoon.
  No.415049 Rfn. Scotton A. states:-
They went off but did not meet anybody until we came to a place with wire round it. We went inside on the left of the wire In front there was a swamp. One of the men was knocked over and we came out and had to retire a little on account of the stick grenades dropping near us. The order passed was to retire in threes. I looked round and saw the others going back and I went back after them. I dropped into shell holes and waited until dark and eventually got in touch with the 2/2nd Bn.
Lieut. MARSHALL and 22 O.R. went into action. 5 wounded, 7 killed, 5 missing, 5 returned. Lieut. MARSHALL missing.

No.15 platoon.
  No.390693 Sgt. Canner F. states:-
We went out behind 13 platoon. We were told to go about 200 yds slightly to our left. 14 platoon had to go to VALE HOUSE. We pushed on and tried to give them support as we expected them to meet with resistance there. We found nothing that represented VALE HOUSE but went on well beyond where I thought it would be. Then I told them to drop into shell holes and tried to find out where we were when it got lighter. I saw somebody in front with our hats on and went towards them. It turned out to be Mr MARSHALL with 14 platoon. He asked me what I thought the direction was as he thought he was wrong and I thought I was wrong, and thought we had come too far. I thought we had to be a bit more to the left. He asked me what I was going to do and I said "hang on until it was light when I would try to find out where we were" He went a little left and then worked round my left flank and retired to my rear which is the last I saw of him. We stayed in the shell holes until 4 in the afternoon, our barrage having been on since 1. We made back from shell hole to shell hole going west and quite by accident struck 16 platoon and established a line with them. I sent back to Bn. H.Q. to give information but found Coy. H.Q.
22 went into action.- 2 killed, 6 wounded, 1 missing, 13 returned.

No.16 platoon.
  No.390929 Sgt. Walker G.G. states:-
We started off and kept due east. I carried on and went about 300 yards xxxxxxxxxxxxxxxxxxxxxxx. I then dug in. We were fired at from the extreme left which I imagined was coming over the STROMBEEK. While there a few men cleared out of the mist. They were 14 platoon. I asked them what was going on in the front. They said they had order to retire by 3s. I thought perhaps I would keep a watch in case they were driven back and we remained xxxxxxx in that position for a long time. Ultimately our own barrage fell very near and I gradually had to retire by sections. I gradually fell back to within 100 yards of where we started from.
There were not more than 50 yards away on my left some small

buildings which were unoccupied. I fell back with my left flank ultimately near STROPP FARM about 50 yards in advance of the forming up line. We kept having wounded men coming through all night from one place and another.

Total number of "D" Coy. going into action - 3 Officers 109 O.R.
Total Casualties -   1 Officer 50 O.R.

Sec. Lieut. G. SPENCER-PRYSE states:-
We formed up on the tapes-Nos. 11 and 9 platoons in front with Mr BROWETT in charge. I was in charge of 10 and 12 platoons immediately behind. Orders were to advance 75 paces behind the leading platoons.

No. 11 platoon.
Rfn. Williams states:-
I was on the extreme right of the platoon with Mr BROWETT and the Lewis Gun section. We went forward as far as I can judge about 120 yards. We came across some barbed wire. We worked round to the right of this wire to the other side. We lost the other section who must have gone to the left. We kept straight on working round to the centre of the wire to get into position. We could not see any sign of any other sections, nobody on our right or left. We got out about 60 yards in front of the wire and stayed in a shell hole. We saw the Germans retiring from the place and about half an hour afterwards started coming back again. Mr BROWETT said we had gone beyond our position. After that we got to the shell hole. We ran out 5 tapes. Mr BROWETT reckoned we had gone 100 yards from the end of the tape. I was with Mr BROWETT when he was killed. He was killed in a shell hole - shot by a sniper. There were 9 including the officer when we got to the shell hole. The remainder were to our left and we lost them in the mist. The only people we saw after that were 2 stretcher bearers some distance to our right. We never saw any more of our other men. The Germans were formed up ready to counter-attack, they brought up a machine gun and Mr BROWETT shot the two gunners and damaged the gun. They brought up another gun and Mr BROWETT was going to fire at the gunner when he was killed. Our gun was out of action and Corporal Scillitoe in charge at the time said we had better make for the tape. The Germans were coming down over the ridge. Some Germans to our left were throwing bombs at D Coy. on our left. As soon as Mr BROWETT was killed we came back. The Germans were closing in. Mr BROWETT was killed by a bullet.
18 men went into action. Casualties; 3 wounded 8 missing, 7 men returned.

No. 9 platoon.
No. 393020 Rfn. Wheeler states:-
I was the right hand man immediately next to "A" Coy. We followed the barrage as quick as possible. The barrage got farther and farther away. We followed up to about 150 yards. I stopped 2 German prisoners, searched them and sent them back. I turned round to carry on and found myself surrounded by "A" Coy. and from there carried on with "A" Coy. I saw nothing of "C" Coy afterwards.
23 men went into action. 4 killed, 14 missing, 3 wounded.
2 men returned.

No. 10 platoon.
No. 301954 Cpl. Kingswell T.J. states:-
I was on the tape when No. 9 started. Judging they had gone about 50 yards I sent my first section. I followed about 15 yds behind with L.G. section. Cpl. Port ran out the tape about 250 yds from the starting point, 5 tapes were put out. I went on about another 40 yards which I thought brought me into my position.

I could see nothing of No. 9 platoon in front. I could not see very far. When I got to the end of the tape I knew I had not gone quite our distance so I went forward about 30 yards and saw 3 suitable shell holes to put the men in. I put them in but the Lewis Gun could not get a field of fire. I went forward and found a good field of fire, took the team and established a point there, and I came back and joined the rest of the platoon. There were quite a number of Germans in our direct front. The L.G. was firing at 300 yards. 1 Wounded, 15 returned.

No. 12 platoon.

390542 L/C. Fennell O. We formed up on the left of No. 10 platoon. When the barrage started I took my men over and could see No. 11 in the mist, taking the men forward till we got to the kicking off tape. We laid out 5 lines of 50 yds and took up a position at the end of 250 yds tape which was the objective. I received orders that I might have to retire back a little. I sent out a man to get in touch with No. 10 but he was wounded. Cpl. Chapman tried to get in touch with us but was killed. Germans were half right a long way off. I took up a position and stayed there. On my way to my position I found one or two men of No. 11 and took them under my charge. During the day I saw a man of No. 11 platoon come crawling from shell hole to shell hole who was wounded in the head. He said No. 11 were practically wiped out ✗ I hung on to my position. I hung on to my position until night time when I was to withdraw as well. The order came through from the rear - a stretcher bearer brought it down. We were to retire to a position in the reserve line. I went back to the left of some MEBUS and stayed there one day and one night. No. 11 reached its objective and stopped there.

✗ and were retiring

13 men went into action. Casualties: 1 killed, 3 wounded.

Lieut. HODGKINSON "A" Coy. stated that No. 1 platoon was on the right, No. 2 on the left, No. 3 behind No. 1, No. 4 behind No. 2.

No. 392995 Cpl. Rosenkranz M. states:-

We started off at zero hour on the left to attack AVIATIK. AVIATIK was about 300 yds away. We got well up and seemed to be a little ahead of C Coy, trying to keep on the extreme edge to keep in touch. We got some distance ahead and could see figures across the flank who turned out to be the 2/18th. We were going down hill at this time and seemed to run into a number of Germans who came out of shell holes with hands up. Myself and one other man disarmed them. I could hardly see anyone at all except a bunch of the 2/18th on our right. We took 12 Germans over to the 2/18th and left them there and did not know where we were. It was impossible to take compass bearing. Went on a little further and got into our barrage. I must have been well over to the right and could see no one to the left. There were several MEBUS about. I did not know what Coy. of the 2/18th it was. This was about ½ hour after zero. We could see the barrage when we left the 2/18th. We went left and seemed to walk into the barrage again. There was only one way out which was behind. We came across the M.G. section of the platoon trying keeping off some Germans trying to attack. It was very misty I got them together with me, retired a little further back and then ran into Cpl. French of No. 3 platoon. He had a message from Mr Hodgkinson to Mr Blackburne. The barrage at that time was all round us. Finally we came across Mr HODGKINSON and he kept us with him and we formed a line on the left.

No.1 Pltn Casualties: 1 O.R. killed, 1 officer and 11 O.R. wounded, 1 missing.
2 " " 1 O.R. killed, 4 O.R. wounded 1 O.R. missing.

No. 3 platoon.

No.391934 L/C. Calder A.H. states:-
I saw only my own section. I could not see No. 1. We went

about 250 to 300 yards and as I told Mr BLACKBURNE we were bearing off to our right he tried to take a compass bearing but could not do so. The 2/12th Bn. pushed across our front and pushed us back rather towards our left, finishing up 250 yards (about) slightly S.E. to E. We should have finished up due E.

    Casualties: 1 Officer and 3 O.R. killed, 7 O.R. wounded, 1 O.R. missing.

Captain FLETCHER "B" Coy. states:-

The Coy. was formed up. No.7 on the right, No.6 on the left No.8 behind No. 7 and No. 5 behind No. 6.

No.7 Platoon.

No. 391990 Rm. Garratt H.G. states:-

Our orders were to form up behind the tape and to follow the sergeant on our left and follow "A" Coy until they got their objective. We started off and got to "A" Coy. and went half right from there. The barrage was just in front. I thought one or two of our men were hit by our barrage. We were held up on the right by a MEBUS (CAIRO). There we came into contact with the Rangers. All our NCOs. were wounded except one corporal who said "carry on". We went forward until we came to a place called The NILE on our right. The corporal was wounded there and the officer of No.11 platoon Rangers took over and he told us to go right up on the left and protect his flank. We asked him about our objective and he said "No good, I have not enough men" and I was to go on his left and remain there. We remained there until the counter-attack in the afternoon, and on our right were two or three battalions retiring one after another, and we had to retire until we came to DOM trench, and when the attack was over we went forward once more. We saw no Germans where we were but could see them on our right. The officer had orders to retire on our left. We had Machine guns with us all the time. At night we went forward to our old line and I was relieved and sent back in reserve. There I remained until relief. I came out with the 2/12th. Our names were taken and we were told he would be responsible for us.

    Casualties; 3 killed, 14 wounded. 14 returned.

No.6 Platoon.

No.392601 L/C. Buxton E. states:-

We started off at the correct time and followed our barrage and the leading section of my platoon had instructions to keep in touch with No. 7 platoon. We were following "A" Coy. and we advanced some good way. When we had advanced to what I roughly estimate about 300 yards my platoon commander Sgt. Beer, apparently was looking out to see exactly where he was, he was hesitating, when he called round that he was wounded. We saw no Germans up to then. We were following the barrage fairly closely. The first thing I did was to run to him and pull him down a shell hole and dress his wounds. Then while I was doing that Sec.Lt HARPER of "A" Coy. passed by and asked me who I was. I told him I was 6 platoon of "B" Coy. He said you had better follow me. I, with the men of my section, followed him and fell into a shell hole a little in front of where I left the sergt. There we were being very intensely sniped from our right, left and immediate front, and also under M.G. fire. We stayed there and gathered from Mr HARPER that he had 3 or 4 men of his Coy. in a shell hole immediately in front of ours. Directly the mist cleared we could see Germans standing about and also sniping from shell holes on our right practically about 6 shell holes away. I imagined I was at AVIATIK FARM. We fired rifle grenades at MR HARPER's suggestion into the snipers. I particularly asked him if there were any of our men in front. He said no. We stayed there and seemed to be in a very advanced post. I ascertained later that our No.5 platoon with a machine gun were on our left flank by a little clump of trees

surrounding farm buildings which I imagined was AVIATIK FARM,
We held on there all the time. As soon as it was sufficiently
dark Mr HARPER said he was going back to find Mr FLETCHER and
report. Cpl. Savage and myself assumed command of this position
which we carried on with until we came out.

Casualties "B" Coy.
    1 Officer and 9 OR. killed.
    30 Other Ranks   wounded.
    1   "   "   missing.

Mr HARPER states that he lost his platoon. They went off
too much to the right with the exception of H.Q. and half
the Lewis Gun team.

Missing by Companies.

Coy.	
A Coy.	4
B "	1
C "	15
D "	98

Vol 9 17/35
17/38

Confidential

War Diary

of

2/9th Battalion London Regiment
(Queen Victoria's Rifles)

Period

From 1st October 1917 to 31st October 1917

Volume 1.

Army Form C. 2118.

WAR DIARY
or
INTELLIGENCE SUMMARY.
(Erase heading not required.)

Instructions regarding War Diaries and Intelligence Summaries are contained in F.S. Regs., Part II. and the Staff Manual respectively. Title pages will be prepared in manuscript.

Place	Date	Hour	Summary of Events and Information	Remarks and references to Appendices
REIGERSBURG CAMP	1/10/17		Battalion proceeded to VLAMERTINGHE B.3.C.3.1 & Moved By rail to AUDRUCQ D.9.d.7.0 & thence by route march to Billets at LISTETE&AUX D.26.a.c. arriving 1 a.m. 2nd inst.	Map 5–8 & Map 27A NE
LISTERGAUX	2/10/17		Battalion rested	
"	3/10/17		Parade under Coy arrangements. Inspection by C.O. of reinforcements who joined the Battalion at REIGERSBURG	
"	4/10/17		Company training to include close order drill & artillery formation, also special classes	
"	5/10/17		Company training & special classes	
"	6/10/17		Company training to include close order drill & attack practice. Use of Battn at TECQUE	
"	7/10/17		Church Parade	
"	8/10/17		Battalion paraded & marched to rifle range S.E. of NORTLEULIN & HEM. Carrying out the following practice, 5 rounds application, 10 rounds rapid at 200x, 5 rounds application 15 rounds rapid at 300x	
"	9/10/17		Company training including close order drill & extended order drill. Lewis Gun School proceeded to "B" training area T.84 under the Hodgkinson for practice. Off. Platoon Coms & Platoon Serg.ts paraded for special class of P.T. & B.T. under Staff Instructor. Inspection of reinforcements by E.O.	Map 24 V E

N. P. M.M. Major

Army Form C. 2118.

WAR DIARY
or
INTELLIGENCE SUMMARY.
(Erase heading not required.)

Instructions regarding War Diaries and Intelligence Summaries are contained in F. S. Regs., Part II. and the Staff Manual respectively. Title pages will be prepared in manuscript.

Place	Date	Hour	Summary of Events and Information	Remarks and references to Appendices
LISTERGAUX	10/10/17		Battalion paraded & marched to GWEMY Range for field firing practice	
"	11/10/17		Company training to include attack drill & musketry. O.C. Coys & Signalling Officers discussed sidings from South. Major Miller to prepare for carrying out a Brigade Tactical Exercise. Inspection of reinforcements by Brigadier	
"	12/10/17		Battalion paraded for Brigade manoeuvre on "B" training area. T.24. Dinners in the field	app 24 ANE
"	13/10/17		Battalion parade cancelled owing to weather. Inspection of reinforcements by C.O.	
"	14/10/17		Church Parade. Lewis Gun School proceeded to B Range for firing practice	
"	15/10/17		Battalion marched to B training area T.24 for Brigade manoeuvres making an attack under cover of smoke on the 2/10, 2/11, 2/12 Battns	app 27 NE
"	16/10/17		Coy's practised drill attack formations, forming up on tapes etc. Proceeded to B Range in afternoon & carried out Infantry, 70 rounds rapid at 200⁺, 5 rounds application at 500⁺ application + 15 rounds rapid at 300⁺, 5 rounds application	
"	17/10/17		Coy snipers & observers proceeded to B Range. Battalion paraded for the presentation by the G.O.C. Divcavon of ribbons to Officers & O.R. who had been awarded Medals in the recent operations	

H. P. Miller Major

WAR DIARY
or
INTELLIGENCE SUMMARY.
(Erase heading not required.)

Army Form C. 2118.

Instructions regarding War Diaries and Intelligence Summaries are contained in F. S. Regs., Part II. and the Staff Manual respectively. Title pages will be prepared in manuscript.

Place	Date	Hour	Summary of Events and Information	Remarks and references to Appendices
LISTERBAUX	17/10/17		Lecture & Presentation to Brigade marched past in Columns of platoons	
"	18/10/17		Coys paraded under Coy arrangements & have use of Range at LA MONTAINE every man to throw 3 live bomb, R.G. Section to fire 3 rifle grenades per man. L.G. Section to fire.	
"	19/10/17		Brigade attack scheme in B training area. Batt. made counter attack on the 2/10, 3/11, 2/12 Battn	Map 27 N.E.
"	20/10/17		Training under Coy arrangements	
"	21/10/17		The Battalion proceeded to AUDRUCQ & then moved by rail to Ypres & then by rail & march to ROAD SIDE CAMP. JAN-TEN-DIEZEN. F.25.c.1.4	Map 27 N.E.
ROAD SIDE CAMP	22/10/17		Parades under Company arrangements	
"	23/10/17		Battalion paraded & marched to training Area L.9 for Practice attack. Inspection on return by the Commanding Officer of E. & D. Companies	Map 27 N.E.
"	24/10/17		Battalion paraded & proceeded to training Area for Brigade Operations. Inspection of H.Q. Coy by the Commanding Officer. Battle Surplus under Lieut Harun for inspection by the G.O.C. after which they proceeded to the Byfrost Battn at HOUTKERQUE. E.14.d.83	Map 27 N.E.
"	25/10/17		Battalion paraded Coys parading independently to training area for attack Practice	

W. P. M. Nin
M/MN

WAR DIARY
or
INTELLIGENCE SUMMARY.
(Erase heading not required.)

Army Form C. 2118.

Place	Date	Hour	Summary of Events and Information	Remarks and references to Appendices
ROAD SIDE CAMP	26/10/17		Battalion paraded & marched to training area for Attack Practice. The following Officers made a reconnaissance of IRISH FM 27.a.2.6. CANE TRENCH 9.a.2.2 YARNA FM 4.a.4.2 & track leading to PHEASANT FM 30.b.1.7. Transport Officer, Signalling Officer, Intelligence Officer, Coy Commanders & Commanding Officer.	Maps 28 NW 2 & 28 SE 3
"	27/10/17		Attack Practice conferences at H.Q. the final of Coy Commanders. Inspection of C & D Coys by Commanding Officer. Church Parade.	
"	28/10/17 29/10/17		Battalion Parade for Attack Practice in training area	
"	30/10/17		Battalion paraded 3.45 am. was preceded by train to REIGERSBERG and was billeted in WEST SECTOR YSER CANAL Sheet 28 NW C.25.a 7.7	
"	31/10/17		Battalion paraded at 2 pm and preceded by route march to line, and took over from 174 Inf Bde line from HELLES HOUSE through POELCAPELLE VILLAGE to TRACAS FARM. BN. HQ at NORFOLK HOUSE Sheet 20 SE. V.19.a 6.2.	

W.P. Milton Major

Confidential

Vol 10

War Diary
of
2/9th Battn. London Regiment.
(Queen Victoria's Rifles)

Period from 1st November 1917 to 30th November 1917

Volume 1

WAR DIARY or INTELLIGENCE SUMMARY

Army Form C. 2118.

Place	Date	Hour	Summary of Events and Information	Remarks and references to Appendices
SIEGE CAMP TRANSPORT LINES	1/7/17	night	Transport lines bombed 2 Horses + 2 Mules killed, 6 Horses + 2 Mules injured, 1 O.R. wounded	
"	2/7/17	3 AM 9 AM 11 AM	Battalion on the line "A" Coy holding HELLE'S HOUSE V.14.c.65 + NOBLES FM	
			V.14.d.23 with two platoons of "D" Coy in support at the BREWERY POELCAPPELLE	sheet STREET
			V.20.a.49 "B" Coy holding MEUNIER HOUSE V.20.d.12 "C" Coy holding TRACAS FM	
			V.20.c.45 + the MEBOS, front in front with two platoons of "D" Coy in support at	V.20.a.a
			GLOSTER FM V.20.c.33. Bn HQ at NORFOLK HOUSE V.19.d.63	
"	2/7/17	9pm	Battalion relieved by 2/12 London Regt. & proceeded to billets on the YSER	sheet 20 N.W.
			CANAL BANK C.25.a.65	20 N.W.
CANAL BANK	3/7/17		Battalion resting	
"	4/7/17		Battalion paraded at 3 P.M. & proceeded by route march to KEMPTON PARK	Sheet 28 N.W.
			C.15 L.95 where it was billetted in huts	
KEMPTON PARK	5/7/17		Battalion paraded mounting + carrying parties	
"	6/7/17		" " " "	
"	7/7/17		" "D" Coy took over holding of PHEASANT	
			TRENCH U.30 CENTRAL from a coy of the 2/10 London Regt	Sheet 20 N.W.
"	8/7/17		Battalion provided working parties. "D" Coy returned from PHEASANT TRENCH	sheet 28 N.W.
			by a Coy of the 9/16" London Regt. Battalion proceeded to SIEGE CAMP B.20.d.84	
			by motor lorry	

K.W. Murray
Capt. & Adjutant
O.C. 26 Battn. LONDON R. ST.

WAR DIARY or INTELLIGENCE SUMMARY.

Army Form C. 2118.

(Erase heading not required.)

Place	Date	Hour	Summary of Events and Information	Remarks and references to Appendices
SIEGE CAMP	9/11/17		Battalion paraded under company arrangements	
"	10/11/17		" " " " also change of general instructor	
"	11/11/17		The Commanding Officer inspected the Camp Companies parading in their Coy lorries	
"	12/11/17		Battalion paraded under Company arrangements. The Commanding Officer inspected all Reinforcements	
"	13/11/17		Parade under Coy arrangements "B" Coy visited the Range	
"	14/11/17		The Battalion preceded by route march to ELVERDINGHE B.14.d.94 & entrained for PROVEN F.4.d.94 & thence by rail moved to PURBROOK CAMP W.89.c.25	Sheet 28 NW Sheet 19 SE
PURBROOK CAMP	15/11/17		Battalion Musketeer Instructor the change outfit & equipment in afternoon went for a short route march	
"	16/11/17		Commanding Officer inspected the Companies. Parade under Company arrangements training to include Practice "A" & Platoon & Coy Close Order Drill & Gas Drill	
"	17/11/17		The Battalion proceeded by rail to march to PETWORTH CAMP X.25.d.3045	Sheet 19 SE.
PETWORTH CAMP	18/11/17		Church Parade	
"	19/11/17		Parade under Company arrangements including Close Order Drill, Arm Drill, Inspection of Box Respirators by the Divisional Gas Officer	

Army Form C. 2118.

WAR DIARY
or
INTELLIGENCE SUMMARY.
(Erase heading not required.)

Instructions regarding War Diaries and Intelligence Summaries are contained in F. S. Regs., Part II. and the Staff Manual respectively. Title pages will be prepared in manuscript.

Place	Date	Hour	Summary of Events and Information	Remarks and references to Appendices
PETWORTH CAMP	20/11/17		Parade under company arrangements. Inspection of Rifles, Equipment & Gasmasks under A.T.O.	
"	21/11/17		9.15. Lecture by the Brigadier	See ???
"	22/11/17		Parade under company arrangements. "C" Coy allotted the Range at F.4.a.6.6.	
"	23/11/17		" " " "D" Coy "	
"	24/11/17		" " " "B" Coy "	
"			" " " "D" Coy "	Inspection of
"			Report Platoon by R.Commanding Officer.	
"	27/4/17		Church Parade. Lieut Col Perry Robinson took command of the Battalion	
"	26/11/17		Parade under Company arrangements	
"	27/11/17		The Battalion proceeded by route march via PROYEN & thence by train to WIZERNES & C (short HAZEBROUCK troops) to its billets	
			thence by route march (at COULOMBY H.A. thence HALLINES LUMBRES BAYENGHEM & SENINGHEM	"
COULOMBY	28/11/17		Parade under Company arrangements to improve Alltz	
"	29/11/17		" " including Platoon Company Drill & Skeleton training	
"	30/11/17		" " "A" Company Ranging west of Range	

Wm Johnson
CAPT & ADJUTANT
O.C. 2/9 BATTN LONDON REGT
QUEEN VICTORIA'S RIFLES

Confidential

War Diary
of
The 2/9th Battn London Regiment
(Queen Victoria's Rifles)
Volume 1

Period from 1st December 1917
to 31st December 1917

WAR DIARY
or
INTELLIGENCE SUMMARY.
(Erase heading not required.)

Army Form C. 2118.

Place	Date	Hour	Summary of Events and Information	Remarks and references to Appendices
COULOMBY	1/10/17		Parade twelve company arrangements	
"	2/10/17		Voluntary Church Service. Commanding Officer Inspected billets	
"	3/10/17		Platoon Training & Musketry	
"	4/10/17		" one meeting Regt. Medical Officer Re B.E.F. Corps	
"	5/10/17		" " "	Shot
"	6/10/17		" " "	at FIEFERDINGHE (HAZEBROUCK) 1/10000 Sheet 28 N.W.
"			The Battalion moved by busses to NIZERNES 4.D.7.6. & thence by busses to FIEFERDINGHE	"
SIEGE CAMP	7/10/17		B.1.4.9.5. & Marched to SIEGE CAMP (B20.d.9.3) the following Officers made a reconnaissance S.O.I.O. & commanding officers of the air defences in the area: The Battalion proceeded to KEMPTON PARK C.16.E.2.5. for training in line area	
SIEGE CAMP	8/10/17		Red Dinners. At 3.0 p.m. The Battalion moved up into the line A Coy holding HELLES Ho Y.14.d.85.55 & NOBLES FM Y.14.d.83 also the platoon in support in DECAPPELLE V.20.d.19 "B" Coy holding MEUNIER Ho V.20.b.12 & one Platoon on A SPRIET DOECAPPELLE ROAD at V.20.a.8.B "D" Coy holding TRACAS FM V.26.d.45. Move to Le LEKKERBOTTERBEEK act in support platoon at PLUSTER FM V.20.C.33 Batt HQ of NORFOLK HOUSE V.19.d.62 "C" Coy in support at PHEASANT TRENCH	Sheet SPRIET 1/10000
	10/10/17		Bn Relieved by the 1/18 London Regt on the Nunn. C Coy today were attacked from V/5th Batt. in PHEASANT TRENCH both relief. LEKERBOTTERBEEK.	

Army Form C. 2118.

WAR DIARY
or
INTELLIGENCE SUMMARY.
(Erase heading not required.)

Instructions regarding War Diaries and Intelligence Summaries are contained in F. S. Regs., Part II. and the Staff Manual respectively. Title pages will be prepared in manuscript.

Place	Date	Hour	Summary of Events and Information	Remarks and references to Appendices
	10/12/17		"B" Coy taking over another portion of PHEASANT TRENCH. "A" Coy at KEMPTON PARK, with 2 platoons of "D" Coy. The remaining 2 platoons stationed at VARNA FM (C.4a 57)	Sheet 28 N.W.
KEMPTON PARK	11/12/17		A practice night alarm and move reheard at 7.30 p.m.	
"	12/12/17		Platoon injection made temporary arrangements "B" Coy moved from PHEASANT TRENCH to KEMPTON PARK	
"	13/12/17		Coys set to disposal of Coy commanders. The emphasis cleaning rifles & Lewis Guns	
"	14/12/17		Battalion relieved by 2/12 London Regt. taking over the same post as before	
"	15/12/17		Battalion was relieved in the line by 2/12 London Regt & proceeded to KEMPTON PARK & thence by light railway to READING (B.82d.16) & from there by route march Sheet 28 N.W.	"
WHITE MILL CAMP	17/12/17		PARK & WHITE MILL CAMP (B.11d.75). Parades under Coy arrangements	
"	18/12/17		"	
"	19/12/17		" No in clude General Practice & Sentry Drill	
"	20/12/17		" No in clude Close order drill	
"	21/12/17		" " " " Rifle & Route March. The Commanding Officer inspected Coys & their organization	

C.M. [signature]
See Lt. ???
9TH BATT'N LONDON REGT.
(QUEEN VICTORIA'S RIFLES)

Army Form C. 2118.

WAR DIARY
or
INTELLIGENCE SUMMARY.
(Erase heading not required.)

Place	Date	Hour	Summary of Events and Information	Remarks and references to Appendices
WHITE MILL CAMP	22/12/17		Parades under Coy arrangements.	
"	23/12/17		Church Parade & Memorial Service for Officers, NCOs & Men fallen or taken missing this tour in the Battn. Held here in France.	
"	24/12/17		The Battn. marched out to billets "A" & "D" Coys at KEMPTON PARK, & "B" & "C" Coys at PHEASANT TRENCH.	
KEMPTON PARK	25/12/17		Parade including Phys. Instr. Drill & Gas Drill. The two Coys at KEMPTON PARK carried out musketry on the Ranges. Tour of Defence.	
"	26/12/17		Parade under Coy arrangements.	
"	27/12/17		Coy commanders made a reconnaissance of the front line taking one from H.Q. London Regt.	
"	28/12/17		At 5.0 p.m. the Battn. marched up into the front line. "A" Coy holding HELLES to SHEET Y11 c.0.3.5 & NOBLES FM. V.14 d.20.30 with one platoon in support in BRECAPELLE-YPRES-NY-POSYPREET "B" Coy holding MEGNIER Ho V.20.b.1.2 & one platoon on the SPRIET ROAD V.20.a.8.5 Ypres "D" Coy holding TRACAS FM. V.26.d.4.5 down to the LEKERBOTTERBEEK with a sufficient platoon at GLASTER FM. V.20.c.3. "C" Coy in support at PHEASANT TRENCH	
	29/12/17 - 31/12/17		Battalion in the line.	

[signature] Lt. A/Adjt for O.C.
9TH BATTN. LONDON REGT.
QUEEN VICTORIA RIFLES

Vol. 12

Confidential

War Diary

-of-

9th Battalion London Regiment
(Queen Victoria's Rifles).

from 1st January 1918 to 31st January 1918.

Volume

Army Form C. 2118.

WAR DIARY
or
INTELLIGENCE SUMMARY.
(Erase heading not required.)

Instructions regarding War Diaries and Intelligence Summaries are contained in F. S. Regs., Part II. and the Staff Manual respectively. Title pages will be prepared in manuscript.

Place	Date	Hour	Summary of Events and Information	Remarks and references to Appendices
In the Field	1/1/18		On the night of the 31/12/17 the Battalion was relieved from the line by the 2/2nd London and proceeded to KEMPTON PARK & thence by light railway to READING (B.22.a.16) & from there by route march to BRIDGE CAMP (B.14.d.75)	27 N.W.
BRIDGE CAMP	2/1/18		Employees at the disposal of Coy Commanders. Men to clean clothing & equipment	
	3/1/18		" " Parade the whole refitting & livery drill	
	4/1/18		The Battalion paraded for the distribution of Medal Ribbons by the C.O. after the ceremony the Battn marched past in column of route	
	5/1/18		The Battalion Christmas Dinner	
	6/1/18		Voluntary Church Service	
	7/1/18		The Battn was then moved by bus from EVERDINGE to PROVEN (E.7.c.0.5) & thence by light railway thro' PROVEN to HERZEELE (D.4.d.9.6) & marched to billets at HOUTKERQUE (D.12.c.4)	27 NE
HOUTKERQUE	8/1/18		Lt Col R.G.H POWELL Grenadier Guards assumed command of the Battalion. Parades consisted of company	
	9/1/18		Parades were Coy training	
	10/1/18		Battalion paraded in Column of Route for march past	
	11/1/18		Parades under Coy arrangements	
	12/1/18		The Battalion paraded for inspection of Boots	

5th BATTN. LONDON REGT. (QUEEN VICTORIA'S RIFLES).

Army Form C. 2118.

WAR DIARY
or
INTELLIGENCE SUMMARY.
(Erase heading not required.)

Instructions regarding War Diaries and Intelligence
Summaries are contained in F. S. Regs., Part II.
and the Staff Manual respectively. Title pages
will be prepared in manuscript.

Place	Date	Hour	Summary of Events and Information	Remarks and references to Appendices
HOUTKERQUE	18/1/18		Voluntary Church Parade	
"	19/1/18		The Battalion paraded for Church Parade. Lecture by Div Gas Officer to all officers	
"	15/1/18		Rifle Range at St ACAIRE allotted to Coys	
"	16/1/18		Parades under Coy arrangements. The G.O.C Division inspected transport	
"	17/1/18		The Battalion paraded for Church Parade. Officers to reconnoitre rt Bangor - St ACAIRE	
"	18/1/18		Hrs Tactical Exercise	
"	19/1/18		Parades under Coy arrangements	
"	20/1/18		The Battalion Marched from HOUTKERQUE to PROVEN where it was billetted for the night	
PROVEN	21/1/18		The Battalion entrained at PROVEN & proceeded to VILLERS BRETTONEUX (O.35.c) & thence by	See 62 D
			route march to its billets at LA NEUVILLE (I.33.d.4)	
LA NEUVILLE	22/1/18		Battalion - rest –	
"	23/1/18		Battalion paraded for drill under the Commanding Officer	
"	23/1/18		" " " " " " Special classes for Drills, Musketry	
"			& Manœuvres from 12 noon to 1 p.m.	
"	24/1/18		Battalion paraded for drill under the Commanding Officer. Special class as before	
"	25/1/18		" " " " " Inspection by the " " "	

Army Form C. 2118.

WAR DIARY
or
INTELLIGENCE SUMMARY.
(Erase heading not required.)

Instructions regarding War Diaries and Intelligence Summaries are contained in F. S. Regs., Part II. and the Staff Manual respectively. Title pages will be prepared in manuscript.

Place	Date	Hour	Summary of Events and Information	Remarks and references to Appendices
LA NEUVILLE	26/1/18		"A" & "B" Coys allotted the Range at H.36.d.89. C&D Coys parade for drill and Battⁿ Parade	General Pamph. Part 62 D
	27/1/18		Church Parade at LA NEUVILLE SCHOOL	
	28/1/18		Lecture of Bone Respirator by the Gas Officer. Lay Lewis Gun allotted the Range	
	29/1/18		All Coys on the Range	
	"		Lewis Gun Section to practice Anti-Aircraft Shooting. Snipers & Observers	
	30/1/18		No more officers & practice	
	31/1/18		"A" & "B" Coys attack the Range. "C" & "D" Training under Coy arrangements	

www.ingramcontent.com/pod-product-compliance
Lightning Source LLC
Chambersburg PA
CBHW081453160426
43193CB00013B/2462